COOKING
FOR ONE

Photography by Peter Barry
Designed by Claire Leighton and
Helen Johnson
Edited by Jillian Stewart and Kate Cranshaw

3567
© 1994 Coombe Books
This edition published 1994
for Parragon Book Service Ltd., Unit 13-17, Avonbridge Trading Estate,
Atlantic Road, Avonmouth, Bristol BS11 9QD
Printed in Hong Kong
ISBN 1-85813-573-7

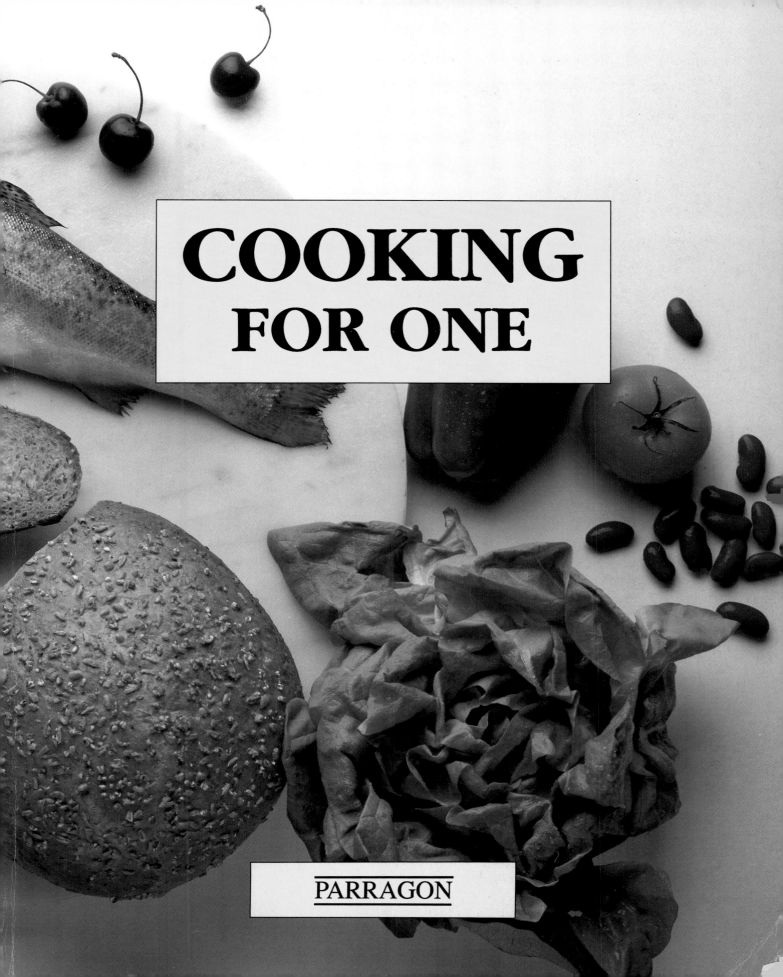

COOKING
FOR ONE

PARRAGON

Contents

Introduction

There is a great skill in cooking for one. It is too easy not to bother, but just to grab a sandwich and a piece of cake, or a piece of cheese and an apple. Sometimes this is all right and is the appropriate thing to do, but it is not always good for the morale, and can lead to a poor and very dull diet.

There is a side to cooking that is therapeutic and comforting. There is the planning involved, the shopping, the preparation, and finally the eating and enjoyment of something thoughtfully made. Just because there is only one of you – whether you are a student, single, widow or widower – it does not mean that it is not worth the effort cooking. Quite the reverse. Cooking and eating good food is a pleasure which adds a new dimension to the day.

There are certain aspects of our high-tech modern world that actually make it far easier to shop and cook for one than ever it was before. Firstly, there is a greater selection of foods than ever before. There are fruit and vegetables, meat and fish, and spices and grains from all over the world. Electronic tills in the shops enable the shopper to buy small amounts, such as two or three items of fruit, or a single head of broccoli, a couple of mushrooms, or a small portion from the delicatessen counter. Also, once home with the shopping, the microwave can be of tremendous help, particularly when cooking vegetables and reheating dishes made previously. It was always such a shame, in the pre-microwave era, when yesterday's moist and succulent fish pie became dry and uninteresting after lengthy reheating in the oven. Of course, the freezer has obvious advantages for the single person, too. Delicious bakes, risottos and casseroles can be made, divided into single portions and frozen for individual use.

People cooking for themselves generally do not want to spend too long preparing their meals, and that is what this book is all about. The recipes are easy to follow, simple to prepare, and each one has an extra ingredient or clever method to make the dish particularly appetising. For instance, olives are added to scrambled eggs, lemon is added to sautéed pork, green peppers go into the ham omelette, broccoli is put with beef, and pancakes are filled with apple. Thus, with a rich and varied food supply and modern equipment, plus the recipes in this book to add the final stimulus, those who are cooking for one have no excuse not to eat an interesting and balanced diet.

STUFFED PEPPER

Stuffed vegetables are very popular in Mediterranean countries.

SERVES 1

1 medium red or green pepper
2 tbsps olive oil
¼ small onion, finely chopped
90g/3oz minced lamb or beef
1 tsp chopped fresh dill
1 tsp chopped fresh coriander
Lemon juice
Grated lemon rind
Salt and pepper
15g/½oz grated cheese
30g/1oz long-grain rice, cooked

1. Wash the pepper and place in a pan of boiling water. Parboil for about 3 minutes and allow to drain and cool.

2. Cut about 2.5cm/1 inch off the top and remove the core and seeds. Trim the bottom of the pepper so that it will stand upright.

3. Heat 2 tsps of the oil and cook the onion briefly. Add the lamb and cook until beginning to brown. Add the remaining ingredients and use to stuff the pepper. Put on the top

4. Stand the pepper upright in a small saucepan. Pour over the remaining oil and add enough water to come halfway up the sides of the pepper. Cook for 30-40 minutes or until the pepper is tender, basting often. Remove the pepper to a serving dish with a slotted spoon.

TIME: Preparation takes 20 minutes and cooking takes about 40 minutes.

PREPARATION: Parboiling the pepper helps to speed up the cooking and makes it easier to remove the core and seeds.

SERVING IDEAS: Serve the pepper either hot or cold, with salad.

9

SCRAMBLED EGGS WITH OLIVES

The addition of black olives to scrambled eggs turns this simple dish into a memorable one.

SERVES 1

3 eggs
2 tbsps olive oil
¼ small onion, chopped
1 small clove garlic, chopped
1 tomato, seeded and finely chopped
4 black olives, pitted and finely chopped
Butter
Salt and pepper

1. Beat the eggs and set them aside.

2. Warm the olive oil in a small frying pan, increase the heat to high and cook the onion, garlic, tomato and olives until all the juices have evaporated.

3. Heat a little butter in a small saucepan, add the eggs and cook over a gentle heat, stirring continuously with a wooden spoon.

4. Once the eggs are cooked, stir in the tomato and olive mixture. Heat through and serve immediately.

TIME: Preparation takes about 10 minutes and cooking takes 15 minutes.

SERVING IDEAS: Delicious with hot toast or muffins. Serve with salad and a French stick for a light meal.

PRAWN AND PINEAPPLE SALAD

This makes a lovely summer meal and the combination of flavours is superb.

SERVES 1

120g/4oz cooked, peeled prawns

900g/3oz seedless green grapes, halved if large

1 stick celery, thinly sliced on diagonal

1 tbsp toasted flaked almonds

30g/1oz canned water chestnuts, sliced or diced

60g/2oz fresh lychees, peeled

1 small can pineapple rings, in natural juice

Chinese leaves or chicory, to serve

75ml/5 tbsps mayonnaise

1 tsp honey

1 tsp light soy sauce

2 tsps mild curry powder

Lime juice, to taste

1. Combine the prawns, grapes, celery, almonds, water chestnuts and lychees in a large bowl.

2. Drain the pineapple and cut the rings into bite-size pieces. Add to the prawns and toss to mix.

3. If using Chinese leaves, shred the leafy part finely, saving the thicker ends of the leaves for other use. Place the Chinese leaves on salad plates.

4. If using chicory, separate the leaves and arrange them whole.

5. Mix the remaining ingredients together thoroughly, to make a dressing. Pile the salad ingredients onto the leaves and spoon over some of the dressing, leaving the ingredients showing. Serve remaining dressing separately.

TIME: Preparation takes about 15 minutes.

VARIATION: Other seafood may be substituted for the prawns.

13

HAM AND GREEN PEPPER OMELETTE

Omelette makes a quick and satisfying lunch dish.

MAKES 1

---

3 eggs
2 tbps milk
Freshly ground black pepper
1 tbsp vegetable oil
30g/1oz chopped green pepper
2 tomatoes, skinned, seeded and roughly
   chopped
60g/2oz lean ham, cut into small dice

---

1. Break the eggs into a bowl and beat in the milk and pepper.

2. Heat the oil in an omelette pan and sauté the green pepper until it is just soft. Stir in the tomatoes and the ham. Heat through for 1 minute.

3. Pour the egg mixture into the frying pan over the vegetables. Stir the mixture briskly with a wooden spoon, until it begins to cook.

4. As the egg begins to set, lift it slightly and tilt the pan to allow the uncooked egg to run underneath.

5. When the egg on top is still slightly creamy, fold the omelette in half and slide it onto a serving plate. Serve immediately.

TIME: Preparation takes about 10 minutes, cooking takes 5 minutes.

SERVING IDEA: Serve the omelette with a crisp leaf salad and French bread.

COOK'S TIP: To skin tomatoes easily, cut a small cross into the skin and drop them into boiling water for about 30 seconds, then plunge into cold water. This loosens the skin.

VARIATION: Use any selection of your favourite vegetables.

CHICKEN AND AVOCADO SALAD

The creamy herb dressing complements this easy summer salad.

SERVES 1

2 anchovy fillets, soaked in milk, rinsed, dried and finely chopped
½ spring onion, finely chopped
1½ tsps finely chopped fresh tarragon
2 tsps finely chopped chives
1 tbsp finely chopped parsley
60ml/4 tbsps mayonnaise
2 tbsps natural yogurt
1¼ tsps tarragon vinegar
Pinch sugar and cayenne pepper
Few lettuce leaves
120g/4oz cooked chicken
½ small avocado, peeled and sliced or cubed
Lemon juice

1. Combine all the ingredients, except the lettuce, chicken, avocado and lemon juice, in a bowl. Work the ingredients until well mixed. Leave in the refrigerator at least 1 hour for the flavours to blend.

2. Shred the lettuce or tear into bite-size pieces and arrange on a serving plate.

3. Top the lettuce with the cooked chicken cut into strips or cubes.

4. Spoon the dressing over the chicken. Brush the avocado slices or toss the cubes with lemon juice and garnish the salad. Serve any remaining dressing separately.

TIME: Preparation takes about 30 minutes.

PREPARATION: The dressing may be prepared ahead of time and kept in the refrigerator for a day or two.

SERVING IDEAS: The dressing may be served as a dip for vegetable crudités or with a tossed salad.

CURRIED PRAWN SALAD

This fish salad makes a quick and tasty lunch.

SERVES 1

1 tsp tomato purée
Squeeze of lemon juice
½ tsp curry powder
2–3 tbsps mayonnaise
120g/4oz shelled prawns
Few lettuce leaves
1 hard-boiled egg, sliced
Few slices cucumber
1 small tomato, sliced

1. Blend the tomato purée, lemon juice and curry powder into the mayonnaise. Fold in prawns.

2. Arrange a few lettuce leaves on a serving plate and pile the prawn mixture into the centre.

3. Garnish with the sliced, hard-boiled egg, cucumber and tomato.

TIME: Preparation takes about 10 minutes.

VARIATION: Use shredded cooked chicken instead of prawns. A mixture of yogurt and mayonnaise can be used if preferred.

SERVING IDEA: Serve with buttered slices of wholemeal bread.

TAGLIATELLE CARBONARA

A classic Italian favourite that is simply delicious.

SERVES 1

1 tbsp olive oil
60g/2oz streaky bacon rashers, rind
   removed, and shredded
Pinch of paprika
2 tbsps single cream
1 egg
30g/1oz Parmesan cheese, grated
120g/4oz tagliatelle
15g/½oz butter or margarine
Salt and pepper

1. Heat oil in a frying-pan, add the bacon, and cook over a moderate heat until beginning to brown.

2. Add the paprika and cook for 1 minute. Add the cream and stir.

3. Beat the egg and grated cheese together.

4. Meanwhile, cook the tagliatelle in lots of boiling, salted water for 10 minutes, or until 'al dente'. Drain, return to the pan with the butter and black pepper, and toss.

5. Add the bacon mixture and egg mixture, and toss together. Add salt to taste. Serve immediately.

TIME: Preparation takes 10 minutes, cooking takes 15 minutes.

SERVING IDEA: This dish is superb served simply with an Italian bread such as Ciabatta.

PREPARATION: The pasta should be very hot when you add the egg mixture to help cook it.

FARFALLE WITH BEEF, MUSHROOM AND SOURED CREAM

This is a great mid-week meal, as it is quick and easy to prepare.

SERVES 1

120g/4oz fillet or rump steak, sliced
30g/1oz unsalted butter
½ small onion, sliced
60g/2oz mushrooms, sliced
1 tbsp flour
60ml/4 tbsps soured cream
5 green olives, pitted and chopped
Salt and pepper
120g/4oz farfalle (pasta bows)

Garnish
Soured cream
1 tsp chopped parsley

1. With a very sharp knife, cut the meat into narrow, short strips. Heat half the butter in a frying pan and sauté the meat over a high heat until well browned. Set aside.

2. Heat the remaining butter in a saucepan, and gently sauté the onion until soft and just beginning to colour.

3. Add the mushrooms, and cook for 2-3 minutes. Stir in the flour and continue cooking for a further 3 minutes.

4. Gradually stir in the soured cream. When fully incorporated, add the meat, olives, and salt and pepper to taste.

5. Meanwhile, cook the farfalle in plenty of boiling, salted water for 10 minutes, or until tender but still firm. Drain well.

6. Serve the pasta with the beef and mushroom sauce on top. Garnish with a little extra soured cream and chopped parsley.

TIME: Preparation takes 10 minutes, cooking takes 15 minutes.

COOK'S TIP: When slicing the meat ensure you cut across the grain as this helps to keep the meat tender.

WATCHPOINT: Always ensure the pasta is well drained otherwise it will spoil the consistency of the sauce.

MACARONI CHEESE WITH FRANKFURTERS

A hearty supper dish, ideal for cold winter evenings.

SERVES 1

2 frankfurter sausages
120g/4oz macaroni
15g/½oz butter or margarine
25g/¾oz plain flour
140ml/¼ pint milk
45g/1½oz Cheddar cheese, grated
¼ tsp mustard powder
Salt and pepper

1. Poach the frankfurters for 5-6 minutes in slightly salted boiling water.

2. Remove the skins from the frankfurters and, when cold, slice the meat diagonally.

3. Cook the macaroni in plenty of boiling salted water for about 20 minutes, or until 'al dente'.

4. Rinse in cold water and drain well.

5. Melt the butter in a small saucepan. Stir in the flour and cook for 1 minute.

6. Remove the pan from the heat and add the milk gradually, beating thoroughly and returning the pan to the heat to cook between additions. When all the milk has been added, simmer for 2 minutes, stirring occasionally.

7. Stir the frankfurters, grated cheese and mustard into the sauce mixture. Season to taste.

8. Add the drained macaroni to the sauce and frankfurter mixture, and stir well until heated through.

9. Pour the mixture into a warmed ovenproof dish and sprinkle the top with a little extra grated cheese, if wished.

10. Heat the macaroni under a preheated moderate grill, until the top is golden brown.

TIME: Preparation takes about 10 minutes, and cooking takes about 20 minutes.

VARIATION: Use 60g/2oz of chopped grilled or fried bacon instead of the frankfurters.

PASTA PRIMAVERA

Primavera is Italian for springtime, and this recipe certainly tastes its best when tender young spring vegetables and herbs are used.

SERVES 1

120g/4oz pasta shapes
Salt
60g/2oz asparagus
30g/1oz green beans, trimmed
½ carrot, peeled and sliced
15g/½oz butter
30g/1oz mushrooms, sliced
1 small tomato, skinned, seeded and
    chopped
1 spring onion, trimmed and sliced
3 tbsps double cream
Salt and freshly ground black pepper
1½ tsps chopped fresh parsley
½ tsp chopped fresh tarragon

1. Cook the pasta in plenty of lightly salted boiling water for 10 minutes until 'al dente', or as directed on the packet.

2. Meanwhile, trim any woody ends from the asparagus stems and cut each spear diagonally into 2.5cm/1-inch pieces, leaving the actual tips whole.

3. Blanch the asparagus, beans and carrot for 3 minutes in boiling water, drain well.

4. Melt the butter in a large pan and add the blanched vegetables and mushrooms. Sauté for 3 minutes, then stir in the tomato and spring onion.

5. Add the cream, seasoning and herbs and bring to the boil. Boil rapidly for a few minutes until the cream thickens slightly.

6. When the pasta is cooked drain well and add to the pan. Toss to combine all the ingredients through and serve immediately.

TIME: Preparation takes about 15 minutes, cooking time is about 20 minutes.

SERVING IDEAS: Serve with garlic bread and a tomato salad.

31

TAGLIATELLE WITH CREAMY LIVER SAUCE

Chicken livers are married with cream and mushrooms in this unusual dish.

SERVES 1

1 tbsp olive oil
½ small onion, sliced
1 small clove garlic, crushed
2 button mushrooms, sliced
150g/5oz chicken livers, cleaned and sliced
2 tbsps single cream
1 small egg, beaten
Salt and pepper
75g/2½oz tagliatelle
1 tsp chopped parsley

1. Heat the oil in a large frying pan, add the onion and garlic and cook gently in the oil until softened.

2. Add the mushrooms and cook for 3 minutes. Add the chicken livers to the onions and mushrooms, and cook until lightly browned.

3. Remove from the heat and stir in the cream. Return to a low heat and cook, uncovered, for further 2 minutes.

4. Remove from the heat and stir in the lightly beaten egg. Season with salt and pepper to taste.

5. Meanwhile, cook the tagliatelle in plenty of boiling, salted water for 10 minutes, or until 'al dente'.

6. Drain the tagliatelle well and toss in the olive oil and black pepper. Serve the sauce over the tagliatelle and sprinkle with the parsley.

TIME: Preparation takes 10 minutes, cooking takes 15 minutes.

WATCHPOINT: Be careful not to over-cook the livers as they will toughen.

PASTA SHELLS WITH MUSHROOM SAUCE

Pasta and mushrooms combine perfectly in this simple dish.

SERVES 1

60g/2oz button mushrooms
15g/½oz butter or margarine
1 tbsp flour
140ml/ ¼ pint milk
Salt and pepper
75g/2½oz pasta shells

1. Rinse the mushrooms and chop them roughly.

2. Melt half the butter in a saucepan and add the mushrooms. Sauté for a few minutes, stirring occasionally. Remove from the pan. Add the remaining butter to the pan and melt.

3. Stir in the flour and cook for 1 minute. Draw off the heat, and add milk gradually, stirring continuously. Bring to the boil and cook for 3 minutes, stirring continuously. Season with salt and pepper.

4. Meanwhile, cook the pasta shells in lots of boiling, salted water for 10 minutes, or until 'al dente'. Rinse in hot water and drain well.

5. Place in a warmed serving dish, and pour over mushroom sauce. Serve immediately.

TIME: Preparation takes 5 minutes, cooking takes 15 minutes.

COOK'S TIP: Do not rinse the mushrooms too much or they will become waterlogged.

VARIATION: Try some of the more unusual varieties of mushroom now available in supermarkets.

MANGE TOUT WITH PRAWNS

Mange tout, peapods and snow peas are all names for the same vegetable –
bright green, crisp and edible, pods and all.

SERVES 1

1½ tbsps oil
30g/1oz split blanched almonds, halved
60g/2oz mange tout peas
1 tsp cornflour
1 tsp light soy sauce
90ml/3 fl oz chicken stock
1 tbsp dry sherry
Salt and pepper
175g/6oz cooked, peeled prawns
30g/1oz bamboo shoots, sliced

1. Heat the oil in a wok. Add the almonds and cook over moderate heat until golden brown. Remove from the oil and drain on kitchen paper.

2. To prepare the mange tout, tear off the stems and pull them downwards to remove any strings. If the mange tout are small, just remove the stalks. Add to the hot oil and cook for about 1 minute. Remove and set aside with the almonds.

3. Drain all the oil from the wok and mix together the cornflour, soy sauce, stock, sherry and seasoning. Pour the mixture into the wok and stir constantly while bringing to the boil.

4. Allow to simmer for 1-2 minutes until thickened and cleared. Stir in the prawns, bamboo shoots and all the other ingredients and heat through for about 1 minute. Serve immediately.

TIME: Preparation takes about 10 minutes, cooking takes 6-8 minutes.

VARIATION: Add spring onions, celery or water chestnuts, and cook with the mange tout.

WATCHPOINT: Do not cook the prawns too long or on heat that is too high – they toughen quite easily.

GRILLED TROUT WITH PEPPER RELISH

Fresh trout, perfectly grilled, and spicy sweet pepper relish makes an innovative and very special dish.

SERVES 1

Little lime juice and zest
15g/½oz butter, melted
1 filleted trout, unskinned (double fillets preferred)
2 tbsps prepared hot pepper relish
Lime wedges or coriander leaves, to garnish

1. Remove the rind of the lime with a citrus zester and set it aside.

2. Mix a little lime juice with the butter.

3. Place the fish fillets on a grill rack and baste with the butter and lime juice mixture. Place under a pre-heated grill for about 4-5 minutes, depending on the thickness of the fillets. Baste frequently.

4. Pour over any remaining butter and lime juice and sprinkle the fish with a little grated lime zest.

5. Gently heat the relish and spoon down the centre of the double fillet. Garnish with lime or coriander.

TIME: Preparation takes about 20 minutes.

WATCHPOINT: When heating the pepper relish, watch it closely as it has a high quantity of sugar and can burn easily.

SKATE WITH BUTTER SAUCE

Skate is both economical and delicious, and makes an interesting change from everyday fish dishes.

SERVES 1

1 skate wing
1 small shallot, sliced
1 parsley stalk
2 black peppercorns
60ml/4 tbsps vegetable or fish stock
15g/1½oz unsalted butter
1 tsp capers
1½ tsps white wine vinegar
1 tsp fresh chopped parsley

1. Place the skate wing in a frying pan.

2. Add the shallot slices, parsley stalk and peppercorns, then pour over the stock.

3. Bring the fish gently to the boil with the pan uncovered and allow to simmer for about 8-10 minutes.

4. Carefully remove the skate from the pan and place on a serving plate.

5. Remove any skin or large pieces of bone, taking great care not to break up the fish. Keep warm.

6. Place the butter into a small pan and cook over a high heat until it begins to brown.

7. Add the capers and immediately remove from the heat. Stir in the vinegar to foam the hot butter.

8. Pour the hot butter sauce over the skate and sprinkle with the chopped parsley. Serve immediately.

TIME: Preparation takes 10 minutes, cooking will take about 12 minutes.

SERVING IDEAS: Serve with fresh vegetables and new or jacket potatoes.

PREPARATION: When the skate is completely cooked, the fish will pull away from the bones in long strips.

WATCHPOINT: Take care not to burn the butter when heating it rapidly. It should only just begin to brown, before adding the capers and vinegar.

SWEDISH HERRING

*The Swedes adore the flavour of fresh dill and mild mustard. This combination is
all that is required to bring out the full flavour of fresh herring.*

SERVES 1

---

1 tbsp fresh chopped dill
3 tbsps mild Swedish mustard
2 tsps lemon juice or white wine
1-2 fresh herrings, cleaned, but heads and
    tails left on
15g/½oz unsalted butter, melted
Freshly ground black pepper
Lemon wedges and whole sprigs of fresh
    dill, to garnish

---

1. Put the dill, mustard and lemon juice or
white wine into a small bowl and mix
together thoroughly.

2. Using a sharp knife, cut three shallow
slits through the skin on both sides of the
fish.

3. Spread half of the mustard mixture over
one side of the fish, pushing some of the
mixture into each cut.

4. Drizzle a little of the melted butter over
the fish and grill under a preheated hot grill
for 5-6 minutes.

5. Using a fish slice, carefully turn the fish
over and spread with the remaining dill and
mustard mixture.

6. Drizzle over the remaining butter and
grill for a further 5-6 minutes, or until the
fish is thoroughly cooked.

7. Sprinkle the fish with black pepper and
serve garnished with the dill sprigs and
lemon wedges.

TIME: Preparation takes 10 minutes, cooking takes 12-15 minutes.

VARIATION: Use mackerel instead of the herring in this recipe.

SERVING IDEA: Serve with new potatoes and green vegetables.

PLAICE AND MUSHROOM TURNOVER

This delicious individual pie makes a warming lunch or supper dish.

SERVES 1

1 plaice fillet, skinned
Salt and pepper
120ml/4 fl oz milk
30g/1oz button mushrooms, trimmed and
  thinly sliced
Butter
Lemon juice
1 tbsp hazelnut, or lemon stuffing mix or
  breadcrumbs
90g/3oz puff pastry
Beaten egg, for glazing
Poppy seeds, for sprinkling

1. Season the plaice fillet and roll it up swiss roll fashion. Secure the roll with a wooden cocktail stick and poach gently in the milk for about 10 minutes in a small pan.

2. Drain the fish and allow it to cool. Remove the cocktail stick.

3. Put the mushrooms and a little butter into a pan with a squeeze of lemon juice. Cook over a moderate heat for about 2-3 minutes.

4. Allow the mushrooms to cool and then stir in the stuffing mix.

5. Roll out the pastry quite thinly into a circle about 15cm/6 inches in diameter. Brush the edges with beaten egg.

6. Put the fish roll into the centre of the pastry circle and top with the mushroom mixture. Pull the pastry edges up and over the fish and pinch together to seal.

7. Place the turnover on a greased baking sheet and glaze with the beaten egg. Sprinkle with a few poppy seeds.

8. Bake in an oven preheated to 200°C/400°F/Gas Mark 6, for about 25 minutes, or until well risen, puffed and golden. Serve piping hot.

TIME: Preparation will take about 20 minutes, plus the cooling time. Cooking will take about 25 minutes.

VARIATION: Make the turnover with wholemeal puff pastry for an even more nutritious dish.

SERVING IDEAS: Serve with new or creamed potatoes and a salad or green vegetable.

SPICED SALMON STEAK

A blend of spices and sugar makes this easy-to-prepare dish very out of the ordinary.

SERVES 1

30g/1oz soft light brown sugar
¾ tsp ground allspice
¾ tsp mustard powder
¾ tsp grated fresh ginger
1 salmon steak, 2.5cm/1-inch thick
1 mini cucumber
2-3 spring onions
15g/½oz butter
1 tsp lemon juice
½ tsp chopped fresh dill
¾ tsp chopped fresh parsley
Salt and pepper

1. Mix the sugar and spices together and rub the mixture into the surface of both sides of the salmon steak. Allow the salmon steak to stand for at least 1 hour in the refrigerator.

2. Meanwhile prepare the vegetables. Peel the cucumber and cut into quarters lengthways. Remove the seeds and cut each quarter into 2.5cm/1-inch pieces.

3. Trim the roots from the spring onions and cut off most of the green tops.

4. Put the cucumber and spring onions into a saucepan, along with the butter, lemon juice, dill, parsley and seasoning. Cook over a moderate heat for about 10 minutes, or until the cucumber is tender and turning transluscent.

5. Put the salmon steak under a preheated moderate grill and cook for about 5-6 minutes on each side.

6. Serve with the cucumber and spring onion accompaniment.

TIME: Preparation takes about 15 minutes, plus 1 hour standing time and cooking takes 12-15 minutes.

VARIATION: Substitute cod or haddock steaks for the salmon.

Truite Meunière aux Herbes

The miller (meunier) caught trout fresh from the mill stream and his wife used the flour which was on hand to dredge them with, or so the story goes.

SERVES 1

---

1 trout, cleaned and trimmed
Flour
Salt and pepper
30g/1oz butter
1 tsp lemon juice
2 tsps chopped fresh herbs such as parsley,
    chervil, tarragon, thyme or marjoram
Lemon wedges, to garnish

---

1. Trim the trout tail to make it more pointed. Rinse the trout well.

2. Dredge the trout with flour and shake off the excess. Season with salt and pepper. Heat half the butter in a frying pan and, when foaming, add the trout.

3. Cook over fairly high heat on both sides to brown evenly. Depending on size, the trout should take 5-8 minutes per side to cook. The dorsal fin will pull out easily when the trout is cooked. Remove the trout to a serving dish and keep warm.

4. Wipe out the pan and add the remaining butter. Cook over a moderate heat until beginning to brown, then add the lemon juice and herbs. When the lemon juice is added, the butter will bubble up and sizzle. Pour immediately over the fish and serve with lemon wedges.

TIME: Preparation takes 10 minutes, cooking takes 5-8 minutes per side for the fish and about 5 minutes to brown the butter.

PREPARATION: If the trout is coated in flour too soon before cooking it will become soggy.

SERVING IDEAS: Serve with new potatoes and peeled, cubed cucumber quickly sautéed in butter and chopped dill.

CRUNCHY COD

Cod provides the perfect base for a crunchy, slightly spicy topping.

SERVES 1

1 cod fillet
Salt and pepper
30g/1oz butter, melted
30g/1oz dry breadcrumbs
¼ tsp dry mustard
¼ tsp crushed garlic
Dash Worcestershire sauce and Tabasco
½ tbsp lemon juice
1 tsp finely chopped parsley

1. Season the fish fillet with salt and pepper and place on a grill pan. Brush with some of the butter and cook under a medium preheated grill for about 5 minutes.

2. Combine the remaining butter with the breadcrumbs, mustard, garlic, Worcestershire sauce, Tabasco, lemon juice and parsley.

3. Spoon the mixture carefully on top of the fish fillet, covering it completely. Press down lightly to pack the crumbs into place. Grill for a further 5-7 minutes, or until the top is lightly browned and the fish flakes easily.

TIME: Preparation takes about 15 minutes and cooking takes about 12 minutes.

PAN-BLACKENED FISH

This Cajun recipe from America uses a spice mixture which is very hot, so use less if you want.

SERVES 1

60g/2oz unsalted butter
1 fish fillet, about 225g/8oz in weight
¾ tsp paprika
¼ tsp garlic granules
¼ tsp cayenne pepper
½ tsp salt and some ground pepper
¼ tsp dried thyme

---

1. Melt the butter, pour about half into a ramekin dish and set aside.

2. Brush the fish fillet liberally on both sides with the remaining butter.

3. Mix together the spices and thyme and sprinkle generously on each side of the fillet, patting it on by hand.

4. Heat a frying pan and add about 15g/½oz butter. When the butter is hot, add the fish, skin side down first.

5. Turn the fish over when the underside is very brown and repeat with the second side. Add more butter if necessary.

6. Cook until the top side of the fish is very dark brown. Serve the fish immediately with the dish of butter for dipping.

TIME: Preparation takes about 15 minutes and cooking takes about 2 minutes per side for the fish.

VARIATION: Use whatever variety of fish fillet or steak you like but make sure it is about 2cm/¾-inch thick.

PREPARATION: The fish should be very dark brown on the top and the bottom before serving. Leave at least 2 minutes before attempting to turn the fish over.

CHICKEN AND SAUSAGE RISOTTO

This is really a one pot meal and one you won't have to cook in the oven.

SERVES 1

15g/½oz butter or margarine
½ small onion, roughly chopped
1 stick celery, roughly chopped
½ small green pepper, roughly chopped
1 small clove garlic, crushed
Salt and pepper
60g/2oz uncooked rice
1 small chicken breast, skinned, boned, and
    cut into cubes
90g/3oz canned tomatoes
30g/1oz smoked sausage, cut into 1.25cm/
    ½-inch dice
200ml/7 fl oz chicken stock
Chopped parsley

1. Melt the butter or margarine in a large saucepan and add the onion. Cook slowly to brown and then add the celery, green pepper and garlic and cook briefly.

2. Add the salt and pepper and the rice, stirring to mix well. Add the chicken, tomatoes, sausage and stock and mix well.

3. Bring to the boil, then reduce the heat to simmering and cook for about 20-25 minutes, stirring occasionally until the chicken is done and the rice is tender. The rice should have absorbed most of the liquid by the time it has cooked.

TIME: Preparation takes about 25 minutes and cooking takes about 20-25 minutes.

PREPARATION: Check the level of liquid occasionally as the rice is cooking and add more water or stock as necessary. If there is a lot of liquid left and the rice is nearly cooked, uncover the pan and boil rapidly.

SERVING IDEAS: Add a green salad to make a complete meal.

CORNED BEEF HASH

The addition of cooked beetroot gives this dish a dash of colour.

SERVES 1

175g/6oz canned corned beef
1 medium boiled potato, roughly chopped
½ small onion, finely chopped
Salt, pepper and nutmeg
1 medium cooked beetroot, peeled and
    diced
15g/½oz butter

1. Cut the corned beef into small pieces. Combine with all the remaining ingredients except the oil.

2. Melt butter in a frying pan and, when foaming, add the meat mixture. Spread it out evenly in the pan.

3. Cook over low heat, pressing the mixture down continuously with a wooden spoon or fish slice. Cook for about 15-20 minutes.

4. When a crust forms on the bottom, turn over and brown the other side. Cut into wedges and remove from the pan to serve.

TIME: Preparation takes about 20 minutes. Cooking takes about 25-30 minutes.

SERVING IDEAS: A freshly-poached egg may be placed on top of Corned Beef Hash. Serve with a mixture of mustard and horseradish, or horseradish and sour cream.

PORK CHOW MEIN

This favourite Chinese meal is quick and simple to prepare, and makes a refreshing change for a midweek lunch or supper.

SERVES 1

75g/2½oz egg noodles
1 tsp Chinese wine, or dry sherry
1 tsp light soy sauce
Pinch sugar
120g/4oz pork fillet, thinly sliced
1 tbsp oil
¼ tsp grated root ginger
½ small stick celery, sliced diagonally
½ small leek, finely sliced
½ small red pepper, cored, cut into strips
Few canned sliced bamboo shoots
   (optional)
60ml/4 tbsps chicken, or other light stock
30g/1oz frozen peas
¼ tsp cornflour
1 tsp water
Salt and pepper

1. Soak the noodles in hot water for 8 minutes, or as directed on the packet. Rinse in cold water and drain thoroughly.

2. Combine the wine, soy sauce and sugar in a large bowl. Add the pork, mix together well, and set aside to marinate for at least 15 minutes.

3. Heat the oil in a large wok, and add the ginger, celery and leek. Stir-fry for 2 minutes.

4. Add the red pepper and bamboo shoots to the wok and stir-fry for a further 2 minutes.

5. Remove the vegetables from the wok. Increase the heat and add the pork, reserving the marinade. Stir-fry the pork over a high heat for 4 minutes, or until cooked through.

6. Return the vegetables to the wok, mixing with the pork. Add the chicken stock gradually, stirring well between additions.

7. Add the peas and cook for 2 minutes.

8. Mix the cornflour to a smooth paste with the water. Add this to the marinade sauce and stir in well.

9. Stir the marinade sauce into the vegetables and pork in the wok. Mix well until the sauce is evenly distributed and is thickened and smooth. Add the noodles and stir everything together thoroughly in the wok, until it has heated through.

10. Season to taste and simmer for 2–3 minutes before serving.

TIME: Preparation takes about 20 minutes, and cooking also takes about 15 minutes.

VARIATION: Substitute sliced beef or chicken for the pork.

SERVING IDEAS: Serve with plain boiled rice and prawn crackers.

ROGNONS À LA DIJONNAISE

This delicious French dish makes good use of vitamin-rich kidneys. Serve with creamed potatoes.

SERVES 1

150g/5oz lambs' kidneys
30g/1oz unsalted butter
1 small shallot, finely chopped
90ml/6 tbsps dry white wine
30g/1oz lightly salted butter, softened
1 tbsp Dijon mustard
Salt, black pepper and lemon juice, to taste
2 tsps chopped parsley

---

1. Trim away any fat from the kidneys and slice them in half lengthways.

2. Carefully snip out any hard core from the centre using a pair of sharp scissors.

3. Melt the unsalted butter in a frying pan and gently sauté the kidneys, uncovered, until they are light brown on all sides.

4. Remove the kidneys from the frying pan and keep them warm.

5. Add the shallot to the meat juices in the pan and cook for about 1 minute, stirring frequently until just soft.

6. Add the wine and bring to the boil, stirring constantly and scraping the pan to remove any browned juices.

7. Boil this sauce rapidly for 1-2 minutes to reduce slightly. Remove the pan from the heat.

8. Add the softened butter to the pan with the mustard and seasonings. Whisk the mixture into the reduced sauce with a small whisk or fork.

9. Return the pan to the heat and add the kidneys and the parsley. Heat very gently for 1-2 minutes, taking care not to boil the mixture any further. Serve immediately.

TIME: Preparation takes approximately 20 minutes, cooking takes about 15 minutes.

WATCHPOINT: Do not overcook the kidneys or they will become tough.

BEEF WITH BROCCOLI

This recipe uses the traditional Chinese method of cutting meat for stir-frying which ensures that the meat will be tender and will cook quickly.

SERVES 1

175g/6oz rump steak, partially frozen
60ml/4 tbsps dark soy sauce
1 tbsp cornflour
1 tbsp dry sherry
1 tsp sugar
90g/3oz fresh broccoli
3 tbsps oil
1.25cm/½-inch piece ginger, peeled and
  shredded
Salt and pepper

1. Trim any fat from the meat and cut into very thin strips across the grain – the strips should be about 7.5cm/3 inches long.

2. Combine the meat with the soy sauce, cornflour, sherry and sugar. Stir well and leave long enough for the meat to completely defrost.

3. Trim the florets from the stalks of the broccoli and cut them into even-sized pieces. Peel the stalks of the broccoli and cut into thin, diagonal slices.

4. Slice the ginger into shreds. Heat a wok and add half of the oil to it. Add the broccoli and sprinkle with salt. Stir-fry, turning constantly, until the broccoli is dark green. Do not cook for longer than 2 minutes. Remove from the wok and set aside.

5. Place the remaining oil in the wok and add the ginger and beef. Stir-fry, turning constantly, for about 2 minutes. Return the broccoli to the pan and mix well. Heat through for 30 seconds and serve immediately.

TIME: Preparation takes about 25 minutes and cooking takes about 4 minutes.

PREPARATION: Using meat that is partially frozen makes it easier to cut into very thin slices.

LAMB KORMA

One of the best known Indian curries, a korma is rich, spicy and a traditional favourite.

SERVES 1

½ small onion, sliced
2 tsps vegetable oil
Piece of cinnamon stick
2 cloves
1 cardamom pod
½ bay leaf
¼ tsp black cumin seeds
½ tsp ginger paste, or grated fresh ginger
¼ tsp garlic paste, or 1 small clove garlic, crushed
150g/5oz shoulder of lamb, cubed
¼ tsp chilli powder
¼ tsp ground coriander
½ tsp ground cumin
Pinch ground turmeric
2 tbsps natural yogurt
90ml/3 fl oz water
Salt to taste
1 tsp ground almonds
½ green chilli, seeded
Fresh coriander leaves, chopped

1. Fry the onion in the oil until golden brown. Add the cinnamon, cloves, cardamom, bay leaf and the cumin seeds. Fry for 1 minute.

2. Add the ginger and garlic pastes and the cubed lamb. Sprinkle over the chilli powder, ground coriander, cumin and turmeric and mix together well.

3. Stir in the yogurt, cover the pan and cook over a moderate heat for 10-15 minutes, stirring occasionally.

4. Add the water and salt to taste, re-cover and simmer gently for 30-40 minutes, or until the meat is tender.

5. Just before serving, add the almonds, chilli and coriander leaves. Stir in a little more water if necessary, to produce a medium-thick gravy.

TIME: Preparation takes about 15 minutes, and cooking takes about 40-50 minutes.

SERVING IDEAS: Serve with boiled rice, or chapatis.

TO FREEZE: Korma freezes well for up to 3 months, but do not add the chillies before freezing, as the process intensifies their hotness.

PAPRIKA SCHINITZEL

Thin slices of fillet pork are served with a rich tasting paprika sauce for a delicious low calorie meal.

SERVES 1

2 thin slices fillet pork, cut along the fillet

Salt and freshly ground black pepper

1 small clove garlic, crushed

2 tsps vegetable oil

½ small onion

½ small red pepper

½ small green pepper

¾ tsp paprika

3 tbsps beef stock

2 tbsps red wine

2 tsps tomato purée

3 tbsps natural low fat yogurt

1. Trim the slices of pork to remove any fat, and flatten them out with a rolling pin until they are 5mm/¼-inch thick.

2. Rub both sides of the pork fillets with salt, pepper and garlic, then allow to stand in a refrigerator for 30 minutes.

3. Heat the oil in a large frying pan and cook the pork fillets until they are well browned and cooked right through. This will take about 4 minutes for each side.

4. Remove the pork from the pan, set aside, and keep warm.

5. Thinly slice the onion and the peppers. Add to the oil and meat juices in the frying pan, and cook quickly for about 3-4 minutes until they are soft but not browned.

6. Add the paprika, stock, wine and tomato purée to the frying pan with the vegetables, and bring the mixture to the boil.

7. Reduce the heat and simmer until the liquid has evaporated and the sauce has thickened. Season with salt and pepper to taste.

8. Arrange the pork slices on a serving dish and pour the paprika sauce over the top of them.

9. Beat the yogurt until it is smooth and carefully drizzle over the paprika sauce to make an attractive pattern. Swirl it gently into the sauce to blend, but take care not to incorporate it completely. Serve hot.

TIME: Preparation takes 20 minutes, cooking takes about 15 minutes.

PREPARATION: This dish may be made in advance, covered with foil, then re-heated in a moderate oven when required.

COOK'S TIP: If the yogurt is too thick to drizzle properly, whisk in a little water or milk to thin it to the required consistency.

TOMATO BEEF STIR-FRY

East meets West in a dish that is lightning-fast to cook and combines the flavour of a barbecue-style sauce with the texture of a stir-fry.

SERVES 1

150g/6oz sirloin or rump steak
1 small clove garlic, crushed
1½ tbsps wine vinegar
1½ tbsps olive oil
Pinch sugar, salt and pepper
½ bay leaf
¾ tsp ground cumin
1 tbsp oil
1 small red or green pepper, sliced
30g/1oz baby sweetcorn
1 spring onion, shredded

Tomato sauce

1 tbsp oil
½ small onion, finely chopped
¼-½ green chilli, seeded and finely
    chopped
1 small clove garlic, crushed
2 fresh ripe tomatoes, skinned, seeded and
    chopped
1 sprig fresh coriander
2 tsps tomato purée

1. Slice the meat thinly across the grain. Combine in a plastic bag with the next 6 ingredients.

2. Tie the bag and toss the ingredients inside to coat. Place in a bowl and leave about 4 hours.

3. Heat the oil for the sauce and cook the onion, chilli and garlic to soften but not brown.

4. Add remaining sauce ingredients and cook about 15 minutes over a gentle heat. Purée in a food processor until smooth.

5. Heat a frying pan and add the meat discarding the marinade. Cook to brown and set aside. Add the oil and cook the pepper for about 2 minutes.

6. Add the corn and spring onion and return the meat to the pan. Cook a further 1 minute and add the sauce. Cook to heat through and serve immediately.

TIME: Preparation takes about 15 minutes, with 4 hours for marinating the meat. The sauce takes about 15 minutes to cook and the remaining ingredients need about 6-7 minutes.

PREPARATION: The sauce may be prepared ahead of time and kept in the refrigerator for several days. It may also be frozen. Defrost the sauce at room temperature and then boil rapidly to reduce it again slightly.

LAMB IN A PARCEL

Use this quick and easy recipe to make a whole meal in one convenient parcel.

SERVES 1

1 lamb steak or 2 rib chops
Oil
1 potato, scrubbed
2 baby carrots, scraped
½ small onion, sliced
½ small green pepper, sliced
1½ tsps chopped fresh dill
Salt and pepper

1. Heat a frying pan and add a small amount of oil. Quickly fry the lamb on both sides to sear and brown.

2. Cut a piece of foil about 30 × 45cm/12 × 18 inches and oil lightly.

3. Cut the potato in half and place on the piece of foil, cut side up.

4. Top with the lamb and place the carrots on either side.

5. Place the onion slices on the lamb and the pepper slices on top of the onions.

6. Sprinkle with the dill, salt and pepper, and seal the foil into a parcel.

7. Bake in an oven preheated to 200°C/400°F/Gas Mark 6, for about 45 minutes-1 hour, or until the potato is tender and the meat is cooked. Open the parcel at the table.

TIME: Preparation takes about 15 minutes and cooking takes about 45 minutes-1 hour.

VARIATION: Other vegetables may be added or substituted. Use sliced parsnip in place of the carrot. Substitute a red pepper for the green pepper. A pork chop may also be used, and the cooking time increased by about 15 minutes.

SERVING IDEAS: This dish is really a complete meal in itself, but add a tomato or green salad for an accompaniment, if wished.

CHICKEN AND CASHEW NUTS

Many oriental dishes are stir-fried. This simply means that they are fried quickly in hot oil, the ingredients being stirred continuously to prevent them from burning.

SERVES 1

120g/4oz chicken breast, sliced into
    2.5cm/1-inch pieces
1 tsp cornflour
¼ tsp salt
½ tsp sesame oil
1½ tsps light soy sauce
Pinch sugar
4 tsps vegetable oil
1 spring onion, trimmed and chopped
1 tbsp diced onion
Small piece fresh root ginger, peeled and
    finely sliced
1 small clove garlic, finely sliced
30g/1oz mange tout peas
30g/1oz bamboo shoots, thinly sliced
30g/1oz cashew nuts
1 tsp cornflour
1½ tsps hoisin sauce, or barbecue sauce
120ml/4 fl oz chicken stock

1. Roll the chicken pieces in the cornflour. Reserve any excess cornflour.

2. Mix together the salt, sesame oil, soy sauce and sugar in a mixing bowl. Put the chicken into this marinade mixture and leave to stand in a refrigerator for 10 minutes.

3. Heat 2 tsps of the vegetable oil in a wok and stir-fry the onions, ginger and garlic for 1-2 minutes.

4. Add the mange tout and the bamboo shoots to the onion mixture. Stir-fry for a further 2 minutes.

5. Remove the fried vegetables, add a further 1 tsp oil to the wok and heat through.

6. Lift the chicken pieces out of the marinade and stir-fry these in the hot oil for 3-4 minutes, until cooked through.

7. Remove the cooked chicken pieces and clean the wok.

8. Add the remaining oil and return the chicken and fried vegetables to the wok, and stir in the cashew nuts.

9. Mix together the remaining cornflour, the hoisin or barbecue sauce and the chicken stock.

10. Pour this over the chicken and vegetables in the wok and cook over a moderate heat, stirring continuously, until the ingredients are heated through and the sauce has thickened.

TIME: Preparation takes about 15 minutes, and cooking takes 8-10 minutes.

VARIATION: Add a few pineapple chunks into the stir-fry mixture just before serving.

SERVING IDEA: Serve this stir-fry with Chinese noodles.

SAUTÉED LEMON PORK

A perfect way to prepare this tender cut of pork. Butchers will bat out the meat for you.

SERVES 1

2 small pork escalopes or steaks, batted out
    until thin
Flour for dredging
Salt and pepper
15g/½oz butter or margarine
½ small green pepper, thinly sliced
1 small lemon
1½ tbsps dry white wine or sherry
1 tsp lemon juice
3 tbsps chicken stock

1. Dust the pork with a mixture of flour, salt and pepper. Shake off the excess.

2. Melt the butter or margarine in a frying pan and brown the pork. Remove the meat and keep it warm.

3. Add the peppers to the pan and cook briefly, then set aside with the pork.

4. Cut the lemon in half and squeeze 2 tsps juice from one half. Cut all the peel and pith off the other half and thinly slice the flesh.

5. Pour the wine or sherry and lemon juice into the pan to deglaze. Add the stock and bring to the boil. Boil for 3-4 minutes to reduce.

6. Add the pork and peppers and cook for 10-15 minutes over gentle heat. Add the lemon slices and heat through before serving.

TIME: Preparation takes about 25 minutes and cooking takes about 20-25 minutes.

VARIATION: Use red pepper instead of green pepper and add chopped spring onion.

DUCK WITH MANGO

Oven-cooked duck breast, served with sliced mango and coated in a mango sauce makes a delicious combination.

SERVES 1

1 small ripe mango
90ml/3 fl oz duck or chicken stock
1 duck breast
¼ tsp each finely chopped fresh root ginger
    and garlic
Salt and pepper
2 tsps oil
¼ tsp vinegar
1 tsp finely chopped fresh chives

1. Peel the mango. Using a sharp knife, cut the flesh through to the stone in several places all round the mango. Ease away the slices.

2. In a blender, blend the slices from half the mango with the stock until smooth.

3. Rub the duck breast with the garlic and ginger and season with salt and pepper. Heat the oil in a small frying pan and seal the duck all over.

4. Remove the duck from the frying pan and finish cooking in an oven preheated to 220°C/425°F/Gas Mark 7, for 15-20 minutes.

5. In a small saucepan, reduce the mango stock mixture with the vinegar, adding salt and pepper to taste.

6. Heat the remaining mango slices in a steamer for 1 minute.

7. Slice the duck breast and serve it with the hot mango slices topped with the sauce. Sprinkle with the chives just before serving.

TIME: Preparation takes about 15 minutes and cooking takes about 30 minutes.

WATCHPOINT: Cut the mango into thick slices, as they tend to become rather fragile when heated.

LAMB A L'ORANGE

The refreshing taste of orange complements lamb beautifully and this recipe is an ideal way of using up leftover lamb.

SERVES 1

1 tsp oil
1 shallot, finely chopped
½ small orange
1 tsp redcurrant jelly
90ml/3 fl oz stock
Pinch dry mustard
Pinch caster sugar
Pinch of cayenne pepper
1 tsp cornflour
175g/6oz cooked lamb

1. Heat the oil in a frying pan and sauté the shallot gently until soft but not brown.

2. Grate the orange rind, cut 3 fine slices from the orange, trim away the pith and reserve the slices for garnish.

3. Squeeze the juice from the remainder of the orange and add to the shallot, with the orange rind, redcurrant jelly and stock.

4. Bring this mixture to the boil, reduce the heat and cook, stirring continuously for 5 minutes.

5. Blend the mustard, sugar, pepper and cornflour together with 2 tsps cold water, and stir this into the orange sauce.

6. Slice the lamb, add this to the sauce and bring to the boil.

7. Reduce the heat and simmer for 10-12 minutes. When cooked, transfer the lamb to the serving dish, pour a little of the sauce over and garnish with the reserved orange slices.

TIME: Preparation takes about 15 minutes, and cooking takes about 18 minutes.

COOK'S TIP: The sauce in this recipe goes equally well with chicken, duck or pork.

SERVING IDEAS: Serve the lamb with boiled rice and either a carrot, orange and watercress salad, or a green vegetable.

SPICED BEEF

Fragrant and spicy, this delicious Chinese dish is quick and easy to make. Serve with noodles or rice.

SERVES 1

120g/4oz fillet of beef
¼ tsp soft brown sugar
Large pinch anise
Large pinch ground fennel seeds
1 tsp dark soy sauce
Small piece fresh root ginger, grated
Pinch salt
2 tsps vegetable oil
1-2 spring onions, sliced
1 tsp light soy sauce
Freshly ground black pepper

1. Cut the beef into thin strips about 2.5cm/1-inch long.

2. In a bowl, mix together the sugar, spices and dark soy sauce.

3. Put the beef, ginger and salt into the dark soy sauce mixture and stir well to coat evenly. Cover and allow to stand for 20 minutes.

4. Heat the oil in a wok or large frying pan and stir-fry the spring onions quickly for 1 minute.

5. Add the beef and fry, stirring constantly, for 3-4 minutes, or until the meat is well browned.

6. Stir in the light soy sauce and black pepper and cook gently for a further minute.

TIME: Preparation takes about 10 minutes plus 20 minutes marinating, and cooking takes 5-6 minutes.

VARIATION: Add sliced button mushrooms.

SERVING IDEA: Serve the beef with a spicy dip.

GAMMON STEAKS WITH RAISIN SAUCE

The tart and sweet flavour of this sauce is the perfect choice to complement gammon.

SERVES 1

2 gammon steaks, cut about 5mm/¼-inch
   thick
Milk
Oil or butter, for frying

Sauce
1 tsp cornflour
90ml/6 tbsps cider
Large pinch ground ginger or allspice
1 tsp lemon juice
15g/½ oz raisins
Pinch salt

1. Soak the gammon steaks in enough milk to barely cover for at least 30 minutes. Rinse and pat dry. Trim off the rind and discard it.

2. Heat a small amount of oil or butter in a large frying pan and brown the steaks for about 2 minutes per side over a medium-high heat.

3. Mix the cornflour with about 1 tbsp of the cider and deglaze the frying pan with the remaining cider. Stir in the ginger or allspice and the lemon juice.

4. Stirring constantly, pour in the cornflour mixture and bring the liquid to the boil. Cook and stir constantly until thickened.

5. Add the raisins and cook for a further 5 minutes. Add salt to taste. Reheat the gammon quickly, if necessary, and pour over the sauce to serve.

TIME: Preparation takes about 20 minutes with at least 30 minutes soaking in milk for the gammon. Cooking takes about 2 minutes per side for the steaks and about 10 minutes for the sauce.

VARIATION: If wished, cooked ham slices or steaks may be used. In this case, omit the soaking procedure and simply sauté to brown lightly – about 1-2 minutes per side. The cider you use may be dry or sweet. If using dry cider, a pinch of sugar will add to the flavour.

PIQUANT PORK CHOP

The spicy sauce in this recipe completely transforms the humble pork chop.

SERVES 1

1 lean pork chop, trimmed of fat and rind
Oil
½ small onion, chopped
1 tsp brown sugar
½–1 tsp powder mustard
½ tsp tomato purée
½ beef stock cube
140ml/¼ pint water
½ tsp Worcestershire sauce
1½ tbsps fresh lemon juice

1. Grill the pork chop under a preheated hot grill for 6-7 minutes on each side.

2. Heat a little oil in a small frying pan, and sauté the onion gently, until it is lightly browned.

3. Stir the sugar, mustard powder, tomato purée and beef stock cube into the cooked onion. Mix the ingredients together well, then add the water and bring to the boil, stirring continuously.

4. Stir the Worcestershire sauce and the lemon juice into the onion and spice mixture, then check the seasoning, adding freshly ground sea salt and black pepper to taste.

5. Put the pork chop into a small ovenproof baking dish and pour the sauce over.

6. Cook in a preheated oven at 180°C/350°F/Gas Mark 4, for about 40-45 minutes, or until the meat is tender.

TIME: Preparation takes about 15 minutes, and cooking takes about 40 minutes.

TO FREEZE: This dish freezes well, and can be kept for up to 2 months. Freezing should take place before the final cooking period.

SERVING IDEAS: Serve with creamed potatoes and green vegetables.

LIVER WITH ONIONS

This dish is simple to prepare, but absolutely delicious and highly nutritious.

SERVES 1

1 small onion
150g/5oz lambs' liver, thinly sliced
Salt and freshly ground black pepper
3 tbsps plain flour
1½ tbsps vegetable oil
15g/½oz butter
2 tsps fresh chopped parsley

1. Peel the onion and slice thinly, keeping each slice in circles if possible.

2. Trim away any tubes from the liver using a pair of small scissors or a sharp knife.

3. Mix the seasoning and the flour together on a plate and lay the slices of liver into the flour, turning them and pressing them gently to coat all over evenly.

4. Put the oil and the butter into a large frying pan. Heat gently until foaming.

5. Add the onion rings and fry until just golden.

6. Add the liver slices and fry for 2-3 minutes on each side until just cooked. Cooking time will depend on the thickness of each slice.

7. Stir the parsley into the liver and onions and serve immediately.

TIME: Preparation takes 15 minutes, cooking takes about 10 minutes.

VARIATION: Add some shredded streaky bacon with the onions.

WATCHPOINT: Do not overcook liver or any offal, as it will toughen.

BLACKBERRY VEAL STEAK

Veal, with its mild taste, is the perfect background for a rich and flavourful sauce.

SERVES 1

1 veal steak
Seasoned flour
25g/¾oz butter or margarine
1 small shallot, finely chopped
3 tbsps blackberry liqueur
½ small green pepper, thinly sliced
30g/1oz oyster mushrooms
Little chicken stock or water
2 tbsps double cream
15g/½ oz butter, cut into small pieces
Salt and pepper
Fresh, frozen or canned blackberries, for
    garnish (optional)

1. Dredge the steak with some seasoned flour and shake off the excess. Melt the butter or margarine in a frying pan and, when foaming, add the steak.

2. Cook on both sides until browned and then lower the heat. Cover the pan and cook for about 12-15 minutes, or until just tender.

3. Remove the veal steak to a serving dish and keep warm. Add the chopped shallot to the pan and cook until beginning to soften. Add the blackberry liqueur and bring to the boil.

4. Lower the heat and add the pepper and mushrooms. Add enough stock to barely cover, reduce the heat and simmer for about 5 minutes. Pour in the cream and bring to the boil.

5. Remove the vegetables from the sauce with a draining spoon and place them over the steak. Reheat the sauce and beat in the butter, a little at a time. Pour the sauce over the steak and serve garnished with a few blackberries if wished.

TIME: Preparation takes about 30 minutes, cooking takes about 25-30 minutes.

PREPARATION: Beating the butter in at the end makes the sauce shiny and also helps to thicken it.

VARIATION: If blackberry liqueur is not available, substitute blackcurrant (Crème de Cassis). Substitute any other type of mushroom for oyster mushrooms.

SPICY MINCE WITH SPINACH

In India, mince is rarely cooked on its own. Various combinations are used to make it more interesting, and mince and spinach is one of the most popular.

SERVES 1

1 tbsp cooking oil
Large pinch black mustard seeds
¼ tsp cumin seeds
¼ fresh green chilli, finely chopped and
    seeded if a milder flavour is preferred
Piece root ginger, peeled and finely grated
1 clove garlic, crushed
120g/4oz lean mince, lamb or beef
½ small onion, finely sliced
Piece cinnamon stick, broken
Pinch ground turmeric
½ tsp ground cumin
Ground black pepper
90g/3oz fresh spinach leaves, chopped or
    60g/2oz frozen spinach, defrosted and
    drained
¼ tsp salt or to taste
1 medium ripe tomato, skinned and
    chopped
¼ tsp garam masala

1. Heat half the oil in a frying pan over medium heat and fry the mustard seeds until they pop. Add the cumin seeds and immediately follow with the green chilli, ginger and half the garlic. Stir and fry for 30 seconds.

2. Add the mince, stir and fry until all the liquid evaporates – this will take 3-4 minutes. Remove the pan from the heat and keep aside.

3. In a separate pan, heat the remaining oil over a medium heat and stir in the rest of the garlic. Add the onion and cinnamon and fry for 4-5 minutes until the onion is lightly browned, stirring frequently.

4. Add the turmeric, cumin and black pepper. Stir and fry over a low heat for 1 minute. Add the spinach and mix thoroughly.

5. Add the mince and stir until the spinach and the mince are thoroughly mixed. Cover the pan and simmer for 15 minutes.

6. Add salt and the tomato, stir and cook over a medium heat for 2-3 minutes.

7. Add the garam masala, stir and cook for a further 2-3 minutes. Remove the pan from the heat.

TIME: Preparation takes 15-20 minutes, cooking takes about 30 minutes.

SERVING IDEAS: Serve with naan bread and rice.

STIR-FRIED BEEF WITH PINEAPPLE

Sliced fillet steak cooked with pineapple and served in a sweet and sour sauce.

SERVES 1

120g/4oz fillet steak
1 small can pineapple rings, in natural juice
1 tsp oil
1 spring onion, chopped
½ tsp chopped fresh ginger root
1 tsp vinegar
1 tsp sugar
2 tsps light soy sauce
90ml/3 fl oz chicken stock
60ml/2 fl oz pineapple juice, reserved from
    the can
½ tomato, seeded and chopped
¼ tsp cornflour, combined with a little
    water
Salt and pepper

1. Cut the fillet steak into thin strips and season with salt and pepper.

2. Drain the pineapple and reserve the juice. Cut the pineapple rings into small, even pieces.

3. Heat the oil in a wok. Add the onion, ginger and the meat and stir-fry until lightly coloured.

4. Pour off any excess fat.

5. Stir in the vinegar, sugar, soy sauce, chicken stock and pineapple juice. Add the tomato and the pineapple pieces. Reduce the heat and cook for a few minutes.

6. Add the cornflour gradually, stirring continuously until thickened.

TIME: Preparation takes about 15 minutes and cooking takes approximately 30 minutes.

WATCHPOINT: Cornflour can be used to thicken many sauces, but always blend it with a little water first so that it is easily incorporated into the sauce.

FRIED CHICKEN

Fried Chicken is easy to make, and when it's home-made it's much better than a takeaway!

SERVES 1

340g/12oz small chicken portions
1 egg
60g/2oz flour
¼ tsp each salt, paprika and sage
Black pepper
Pinch cayenne pepper (optional)
Oil, for frying
Parsley or watercress, to garnish

---

1. Rinse the chicken pieces and pat dry on kitchen paper.

2. Beat the egg in a large bowl and add the chicken one piece at a time, turning to coat.

3. Mix flour and seasonings in a plastic bag.

4. Place the chicken pieces into the bag one at a time, close bag tightly and shake to coat each piece of chicken. Alternatively, dip each coated chicken piece in a bowl of seasoned flour, shaking off the excess.

5. Heat some oil in a large frying pan to the depth of about 1.25cm/½-inch.

6. When the oil is hot, add the chicken, skin side down first, fry for about 12 minutes and then turn over. Fry a further 12 minutes on the second side, or until the juices run clear.

7. Drain the chicken on kitchen paper and serve immediately. Garnish the serving plate with parsley or watercress.

TIME: Preparation takes about 20 minutes and cooking takes about 24 minutes.

COOK'S TIP: When coating anything for frying, be sure to coat it just before cooking. If left to stand, coating will usually become very soggy.

95

KIDNEYS WITH BACON

Stir-frying is an excellent way of cooking kidneys, as the brief cooking ensures that they do not become tough.

SERVES 1

175g/6oz lambs' kidneys
1 tbsp sherry
2 tbsps vegetable oil
2 rashers lean bacon, cut into 2.5cm/1-inch
    strips
½ small onion, chopped
1 clove garlic, crushed
1 tsp tomato chutney
1 tsp light soy sauce
1½ tbsps water
Salt and freshly ground black pepper
1 tsp cornflour
1 tsp fresh chopped parsley

1. Trim the fat from the kidneys and cut each kidney in half with a sharp knife.

2. Carefully trim out the hard core from the centre of each kidney with a sharp knife or scissors.

3. Cut a lattice design on the back of each kidney using a sharp knife and taking care not to cut right through.

4. Put the kidneys into a bowl and stir in the sherry. Set aside for 15 minutes to marinate.

5. Heat the oil in a wok and fry the bacon, onion and garlic for 3-4 minutes, stirring continuously to prevent burning. Remove from the wok and set aside on a plate.

6. Drain the kidneys and reserve the sherry marinade. Add the kidneys to the wok and stir for 2-3 minutes only.

7. Stir the tomato chutney, soy sauce and water into the wok with the kidneys, then add the bacon and onion mixture. Season with salt and pepper and stir-fry gently for 3-4 minutes.

8. Blend the cornflour with the sherry marinade. Add the parsley to the cornflour mixture and stir this into the kidneys in the wok, mixing well until the sauce is thickened and smooth. Serve at once sprinkled with a little extra parsley.

TIME: Preparation takes 20 minutes, cooking takes 10 minutes.
SERVING IDEAS: Serve with rice and broccoli or mange tout peas.

APPLE FILLED PANCAKE

A light, puffy pancake makes a delicious brunch dish as well as a sweet.

SERVES 1

Filling
15g/½oz butter or margarine
120g/4oz cooking apple, peeled, cored and
    cut into 5mm/¼-inch wedges
1 tsp brown sugar
Pinch ground allspice

Pancakes
1 egg
120ml/4 fl oz milk
15g/½oz plain flour
¼ tsp sugar
Pinch salt
15g/½oz butter or margarine
Icing sugar

1. Melt the butter for the filling in a small frying pan over moderate heat. When just foaming, add the apple and sprinkle with the sugar and allspice. Cook, stirring occasionally, until the apple is lightly browned and slightly softened. Put the apple aside while preparing the batter.

2. Combine the egg and the milk in a bowl and whisk thoroughly. Sift the flour with the sugar and salt and add to the egg gradually, whisking constantly. Alternatively, combine all the ingredients in a food processor and work until just smooth.

3. To cook the pancake, melt the butter over moderate heat in a small frying pan. Pour in half the batter and swirl the pan from side to side so that the batter covers the base.

4. Scatter over the filling and cook the pancake for about 3 minutes.

5. Pour the rest of the batter over the apples and place under a preheated grill for about 1-2 minutes, or until the top is golden brown and firm to the touch.

6. Loosen the sides and the base of the pancake and slide it onto a heated serving dish. Sprinkle the pancake with a little icing sugar.

TIME: Preparation takes about 15 minutes, cooking takes about 5-6 minutes for the pancake, the filling will take about 6-8 minutes.

VARIATION: Grated lemon rind may be added to the filling, if wished. Add more or less sugar depending upon the sweetness of the apple.

SERVING IDEAS: Accompany the pancake with whipped cream or ice cream.

BROWN SUGAR BANANA

Banana cooked in a rich brown sugar sauce makes a delectable dessert.

SERVES 1

1 ripe banana, peeled
Lemon juice
30g/1oz butter
30g/1oz soft brown sugar, light or dark
Pinch ground cinnamon and nutmeg
2 tbsps orange juice
1 tbsp white or dark rum
Whipped cream and chopped pecans, to
    serve

1. Cut the banana in half lengthwise and sprinkle with lemon juice on all sides.

2. Melt the butter in a small frying pan and add the sugar, cinnamon, nutmeg and orange juice. Stir over gentle heat until the sugar dissolves into a syrup.

3. Add the banana halves and cook gently for about 3 minutes, basting often with the syrup, but not turning them.

4. Once the banana is heated through, warm the rum in a small saucepan or ladle and ignite with a match. Pour the flaming rum over the banana and shake the pan gently until the flames die down naturally. Place on a serving plate and top with some whipped cream and a sprinkling of pecans.

TIME: Preparation takes about 10 minutes and cooking takes about 5 minutes for the sugar and butter syrup and 3-4 minutes for the banana.

SERVING IDEAS: The banana may be served with vanilla ice cream instead of whipped cream, if preferred.

COOK'S TIP: Sprinkling the cut surfaces of the banana with lemon juice keeps it from turning brown and also offfsets the sweetness of the sauce.

PASSION FRUIT OMELETTE

A sweet omelette makes a pleasant change from the more usual savoury variety and is best served after a light meal, since it is quite substantial.

SERVES 1

1 passion fruit
3 eggs, beaten
1½ tsps sugar
1½ tsps desiccated coconut

1. Cut the passion fruit in half with a very sharp knife.

2. Place the eggs in a bowl and add the pulp from half of the passion fruit.

3. Add the sugar and coconut and beat all the ingredients together well.

4. Heat a lightly greased frying pan and, when very hot, pour in the egg mixture. Once the omelette is almost cooked, roll it up in the pan.

5. Serve hot topped with the remaining passion fruit pulp, sweetened if necessary with a little sugar.

TIME: Preparation takes about 15 minutes and cooking about 5 minutes.

WATCHPOINT: The oil must be hot before adding the egg mixture in order to seal the base of the omelette immediately.

BUYING GUIDE: Look for passion fruit that are wrinkled, as these are usually riper and therefore sweeter.

QUARKSPEISE

A German speciality, this pudding is a delightfully different combination of pumpernickel bread, soft cheese and tangy cranberries.

SERVES 1

15g/½oz pumpernickel bread made into crumbs
1½ tsps brandy
120g/4oz quark
15g/1½oz sugar
45g/1½oz whole cranberry sauce
½ slice pumpernickel, cut into small squares or triangles, for decoration

1. Place the pumpernickel crumbs in a bowl and sprinkle over the brandy. Stir to coat evenly and leave to stand.

2. Combine the quark and sugar together and mix thoroughly. When the crumbs have softened, fold into the quark.

3. Layer up the dessert with the quark mixture and the cranberry sauce, in a glass dessert dish, ending with a layer of quark on top.

4. Decorate the top with the squares or triangles of pumpernickel and a spoonful of cranberry sauce. Chill before serving.

TIME: Preparation takes about 15 minutes, plus chilling time.

BUYING GUIDE: Quark is a soft cheese readily available in supermarkets and delicatessens.

VARIATION: Other fruit or preserves may be used.

CARAMELIZED PEAR TART

Pear makes a tasty change from apple in this mouthwatering individual tart,
which is akin to the classic French Tarte Tatin.

SERVES 1

90g/3oz puff pastry
1 large pear
2 tsps melted butter
2 tsps sugar

---

1. Roll out the pastry and, using a small plate as a pattern, cut out a round. Place it on a dampened, non-stick baking sheet and prick well with a fork.

2. Peel and core the pear. Halve it and then slice thinly.

3. Arrange the slices of pear neatly on the pastry round. Brush the pear slices with the melted butter.

4. Cook in an oven preheated to 200°C/400°F/Gas Mark 6, for about 15 minutes. When the tart is almost cooked, remove and sprinkle with the sugar. Place it under a hot grill until caramelized. Serve the tart warm.

TIME: Preparation takes about 15 minutes and cooking takes about 15 minutes.

SERVING IDEAS: Serve with caramel-flavoured ice cream.

107

107

LEMON BRANDY CREAM

This rich brandy cream is prepared in minutes and tastes heavenly.

SERVES 1

75ml/5 tbsps single cream
75ml/5 tbsps double cream
25g/¾oz soft brown sugar
Juice and finely grated rind of ½ lemon
30g/1oz sponge cake
1½ tsps brandy
Few toasted flaked almonds

1. Mix the single and double creams in a small saucepan and stir in the sugar.

2. Cook over a low heat, until the cream begins to bubble and the sugar has melted. Stir the grated lemon rind into the cream mixture and allow it to cool in the saucepan.

3. Break the cake into fine crumbs, and place in a serving dish.

4. Stir the brandy into the cream mixture together with the lemon juice.

5. Pour the cream mixture over the cake crumbs and refrigerate for 30 minutes, or until the cream has thickened.

6. Sprinkle the toasted almonds over the top of the cream before serving.

TIME: Preparation takes about 10 minutes, and cooking takes 2-3 minutes.

VARIATION: Use some finely grated orange rind and juice in place of the lemon, and Cointreau instead of the brandy.

SERVING IDEAS: Serve the cream with crisp almond biscuits.

BRIOCHE FRENCH TOAST

This brioche French toast makes an unusual dessert, but could also be served for an extra-special breakfast dish, with or without vanilla custard sauce.

SERVES 1

1 small brioche
1 tbsp double cream
1 small egg
1 tsp sugar
¼ tsp orange flower water
2 tbsps butter
Icing sugar
Vanilla custard sauce, to serve

1. Cut the small brioche into three slices.

2. Beat together the cream, egg, sugar, and orange flower water.

3. Dip each brioche slice into the cream and egg mixture, making sure both sides are coated.

4. Heat a little butter and sauté the dipped slices in a frying pan for about 2 minutes on each side until golden brown.

5. Serve immediately, sprinkled with a little sifted icing sugar and surrounded by the vanilla custard sauce.

TIME: Preparation takes about 5 minutes and cooking takes about 4 minutes.

VARIATION: White bread can be used if brioche is not available.

Index